Me and My Pet

Cats

D1460232

How to train your owner!

Belinda Weber

OXFORD
UNIVERSITY PRESS

OXFORD
UNIVERSITY PRESS

Great Clarendon Street, Oxford OX2 6DP

Oxford University Press is a department of the University of Oxford.
It furthers the University's objective of excellence in research, scholarship,
and education by publishing worldwide in

Oxford   New York

Auckland   Cape Town   Dar es Salaam   Hong Kong   Karachi
Kuala Lumpur   Madrid   Melbourne   Mexico City   Nairobi
New Delhi   Shanghai   Taipei   Toronto

With offices in

Argentina   Austria   Brazil   Chile   Czech Republic   France   Greece
Guatemala   Hungary   Italy   Japan   Poland   Portugal   Singapore
South Korea   Switzerland   Thailand   Turkey   Ukraine   Vietnam

Oxford is a registered trade mark of Oxford University Press
in the UK and in certain other countries

Text copyright © Oxford University Press 2007

The moral rights of the author have been asserted

Database right Oxford University Press (maker)

First published 2007

All rights reserved. No part of this publication may be reproduced,
stored in a retrieval system, or transmitted, in any form or by any means,
without the prior permission in writing of Oxford University Press,
or as expressly permitted by law, or under terms agreed with the appropriate
reprographics rights organization. Enquiries concerning reproduction
outside the scope of the above should be sent to the Rights Department,
Oxford University Press, at the address above

You must not circulate this book in any other binding or cover
and you must impose this same condition on any acquirer

British Library Cataloguing in Publication Data

Data available

ISBN-13: 978-0-19-911582-2

1 3 5 7 9 10 8 6 4 2

Printed in Singapore by Imago

MORAY COUNCIL LIBRARIES & INFO.SERVICES	
20 21 05 43	
Askews	
J636.8	

MEET LUCA

Name: Luca Lewis
Age: 3 months
Breed: Moggie
Lives: Bristol, England
Owners: Paul and Penny Lewis,
             ages 5 and 7

I am writing this for Paul and Penny and their friends,
so that they understand me and we can all live happily together.

Luca

Look at me!

My name is Luca and I'm a tom cat. That means I'm a boy. I'm a friendly animal and I love being a pet. I spend a lot of time dozing, so I need a nice quiet place where I can rest comfortably.

I like to spend time outside, so please fit a cat flap. This means I can come and go as I please and won't wake you up in the middle of the night when I want to go out!

If I rub myself against your legs, it's a good sign. It means I'm marking you as my own!

We cats have very bendy bodies. In this series
of pictures you can see how we move when jumping.
On landing, our back and front feet nearly cross over.

I have sharp **claws** on my front and back feet. I can pull them back into special cases in my feet so that I can creep along silently. The pads on my paws cushion my feet. They help me move quietly.

My **tail** helps me balance when jumping or walking on narrow ledges.

My **back** is very flexible. This means it bends easily.

My **ears** can swivel to pick up sounds. This helps me work out where the sound is coming from.

My **whiskers** are very long. They help me judge how wide spaces are, and whether I can fit inside.

My **nose** is very sensitive and I can sniff out delicious smells, like catnip or tasty treats to eat.

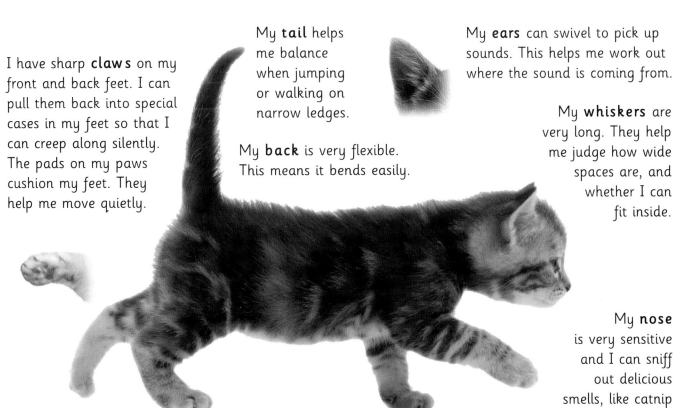

5

Different breeds

I'm a mixed breed cat (a moggie), but we come in lots of different shapes and sizes. Some pedigree cats can trace their families back to the Egyptians! Some pedigree cats are very fancy looking, and can be a bit fussy.

Maine Coons are the largest domestic cat breed. A fully grown tom can weigh up to 11kg. They have long hair and are very friendly. They like their humans and will follow them around.

Persians are one of the oldest breeds of domestic cats. They have thick coats, short legs and a squashed-looking face. They suffer from colds and blocked noses a lot, but are very friendly.

Siamese cats have almond-shaped blue eyes and, short, flat coats. These are very playful, chatty cats. Their cry does sound like a human baby, but don't let that put you off. They are extremely loyal and with a little encouragement, can be trained to fetch things, walk on a lead, and even perform tricks.

Abyssinians are one of the oldest known breeds of cats. They are very muscular and have large ears and almond shaped eyes. They look a bit like the African wild cat, the ancester of all domestic cats.

Who said cats don't like water? They hadn't met the **Turkish Van**! These beautiful cats love water and will regularly take a dip. If they can't get into a pool, they'll stir their water bowls or invent games in the sink. They are intelligent cats and love to follow their humans around.

Birmans are beautiful cats with cream-coloured bodies and darker ears, faces and tails. They have bright blue eyes. They have a very loving nature and are interested in what their humans get up to.

My family

Although I look cute and am easy to pick up and cuddle, some of my relatives are a bit bigger! I'm related to lions, tigers, pumas and jaguars. Some people say this is where I get my proud nature.

Lions are the second largest of all the big cats. They live in family groups called prides. The pride is made up of several female lions, their cubs and one or two males.

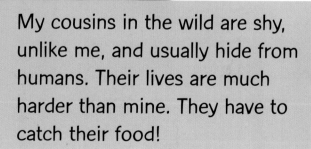

My cousins in the wild are shy, unlike me, and usually hide from humans. Their lives are much harder than mine. They have to catch their food!

Jaguars are big, sturdy cats that live in the rain forests of South and Central America. They like the water and will often cool down in the rivers there.

Tigers are the biggest of all the cats. They live in forests or grasslands where their stripy coats help them blend in with the shadows. They are hunters, and will catch and eat deer, wild pigs and even buffalo. There are not many tigers now.

Pumas are unusual among the big cats in that they cannot roar. They can purr when they are happy and make strange human-like sounds when courting a mate.

I am born

I am very proud and know that I'm important. My mum is called a queen, so that must make me a prince and I certainly behave like royalty!

Just before she gives birth, the queen will look for a suitable quiet spot to give birth. She needs it to be cosy and warm, so offer her a big box with some comfy bedding.

My cousins Joanna, Jonathan and Joel

Baby cats, called kittens, are born nine weeks after a tom and a queen have mated.

We kittens are very wet and messy when we're born, but mum doesn't mind. She licks us clean and tidies our fur so that it will keep us warm. Her tongue tickles us and makes us gasp our **first breaths**.

Kittens are born blind and helpless. We need our mummies to keep us **safe** and **warm** and feed us. We can find her in the nest because she is lovely and warm and smells good.

Mummy lies on her side to **feed** us. We can all find a spot to guzzle down some milk.

Mum gets to know us all and spends a lot of time keeping us clean. I know she likes **washing** us, because she purrs most of the time!

We start eating **solid foods** when we are about six weeks old. Mum stills feeds us milk though. She sits up when she thinks we've had enough but we can still feed.

By the time we are about five weeks old we are **playful** and nosey. We want to chase things and find out what they do. Sometimes we just play for too long, and need a quick **nap**!

Choosing our owners

We can live for up to 20 years, so it's important that we choose our humans carefully. We need to know that our owners will feed us, and look after us properly as well as making a fuss of us when we want it, and giving us plenty of comfy spots to snooze in.

I like to play outside so it's really good if you have a garden. A cat flap in the door is ideal. This means I can come and go as I like.

I do like company and will want to spend a lot of time with my owners. If they have to go to school or are away from the house all day, I prefer having another cat around to keep me **company**. We do need to get along though, so another cat of the same age is best, or one of my **sisters** or **brothers**, like Gordon here.

I keep myself clean and can be trained where to go to the toilet. A **litter tray** is perfect for when I'm very young. Make sure you empty it regularly though, as I don't like to use it if it's dirty!

If I can go outside, my owner can show me how to dig in the soil. Then I'll learn that I can go to the toilet outside too.

I'm very nosey and will want to get into things. Please make sure that I don't hurt myself while **exploring**.

When you have to take me somewhere, I need to travel in a **cat box**. This will need a very secure door as I will try hard to get out.

I will wear a **collar** to help keep fleas off me. Please fit me with one that has a quick release in case I get it stuck while I'm out and about. You can fit a name tag on it with my name and address, so that if I get lost, someone else can let you know where I am.

Some of my friends have **long hair**. They need their carers to **brush** this every day, to stop it getting tangled.

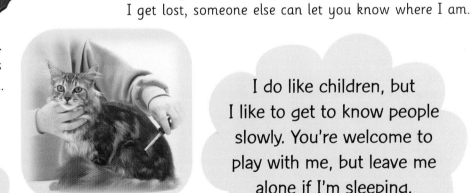

Remember, I will need to settle into my new home. Let me explore one room at a time, so I get used to where things are.

I do like children, but I like to get to know people slowly. You're welcome to play with me, but leave me alone if I'm sleeping.

I'm quick to learn

I love to play and chase things. If you didn't feed me, I'd need these skills to help me catch my food. I will chase just about anything that moves, so please play with me. Cotton reels and ping-pong balls are great to roll around with. And I love anything on a string — try tying a rolled up ball of paper on a piece of string, and I'll chase it.

I have to learn to **trust** people as they are so much bigger than me. It's important that I'm handled gently when I'm getting to know my owners. That way, I'll think of my humans as part of my **family**.

Gordon loves his woollen ball.

If you are gentle with me, I'll let you **stroke** me even when I'm very young.

Throw a pine cone gently towards me, and I'll **catch** it and maybe carry it around in my mouth. I'm pretending it's my prey and that I'm going to eat it for my dinner.

I'll dive into piles of leaves if you let me, to check out the **smells** and also to **chase** things.

As I grow, I'll still like to **play**. Even adult cats play with their carers. I will try to grab your feet as you walk past me or catch your hand and hold it in my mouth. These are hunting skills, but I usually remember not to be too rough.

If you wriggle your toes while you're in bed, I'll pounce on them through the bedclothes.

It's a good idea to give me a **scratching post** made of thick twine — some have catnip in them which I like. I can sharpen my claws without ruining your furniture.

I'm always hungry!

I do love to eat, so please be careful that you don't let me eat too much. I'll get too fat and lazy and won't want to play or run around. I'll let you know when I'm hungry by rubbing around your legs and mewing. If this doesn't work, I'll jump up on any surface and sit right in front of you. That way, I know you have seen me and will feed me soon.

As a kitten, I've developed a taste for milk, but I really don't need to drink it when I'm grown up. If you let me, I'll drink cow's milk, but this can be bad for me and give me a bad tummy. You can buy special cat milk, which is much better for me. Once I'm weaned though, I don't really need milk — I just like the taste.

Mostly I eat **meat**, but sometimes I like to try some **vegetables**. I'll also chew on any **houseplants** that look tasty, particularly ones with long leaves that I can play with as well as nibble. If they aren't good for me, I'm usually sick.

We cats can be **fussy eaters** and go off our food. You will have to learn what things are particularly tasty and what we don't want.

You can buy special **cat food** for me. It comes in different forms – some are dry, while others are meaty chunks in jelly or gravy. They all taste good. Once a tin is open, please keep it in the **fridge** until my next meal to keep the flies off it. I really like it if you let it come to room temperature before you give it to me. It tastes much nicer then.

Dried foods are good because they help to keep my **teeth** healthy. Make sure you give me plenty of **fresh water** to drink, as dried food doesn't have as much moisture as wet.

Sometimes my uncle Walter fancies a different sort of snack and catches a **mouse**. He likes to show it to his owner.

As a treat I do enjoy some fresh meat or fish. Raw minced lamb or beef is lovely and so is lightly cooked white fish like cod or coley. Please take out the bones though. They can get stuck in my throat.

When I'm happy

I'll let you know when I'm happy by purring and rubbing up against you. It shows that I am relaxed and content – although I sometimes do it when I'm begging for food! When I was a tiny kitten, I could feel the vibrations of my mum's purring before I even opened my eyes! This meant that I could always find her when I wanted some food, or to cuddle against her for warmth.

When you come home, I like to come and say hello. I'll **chirp** and **trill** at you and **arch my back** while rubbing around your legs. You'll know I'm pleased to see you as I'll raise my **tail** high. I love it when you chat back to me and **stroke** me.

If I'm resting and you start to stroke me, I'll often murmur that it's ok to keep doing it. This is like a lower version of my greeting trill.

I'll **nudge** you gently with my head if I want your attention. It's my way of saying hello. I like it best when you gently **rub** my head, to show that you're pleased to see me too.

If another cat comes close while I'm resting, I might let it know it's ok by **blinking** slowly at it. It will blink back and we will both relax. You can try this too – make your blinks slow and deliberate and I will blink back at you.

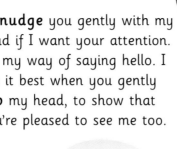

I'll roll and stretch when I'm relaxed. I can get into some very funny positions.

I'll show I'm **happy** to see another cat by rubbing against it. If we know each other well, we'll probably give each other a quick **lick** to make sure we both smell the same.

If I think you're ignoring me, I'll **jump** on whatever it is you're doing and make sure you can see me. I'll lie across your books and **sprawl** over a jigsaw puzzle. It's my way of saying I want you to make a fuss of me.

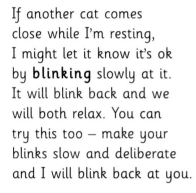

By looking after me well, I can stay **kitten-like** all my life. I love to **roll around** and **play with toys**, even when I'm grown up.

I love to stretch when I wake up. I nearly always have a big yawn first, then stretch out my feet. If I decide to get up, I'll stand tall on my feet and arch my back. Then I move forward a bit for another long stretch. Sometimes I shake out my back legs.

Keep away!

When I'm scared or angry, I'll let you know to keep back. If you don't, I might attack you because I see you as a threat. I can hurt you with my sharp teeth and claws, so please watch out for my warning signs.

I'll let you know when I'm angry by pulling my ears back against my head. I'll open my mouth and make a scary hissing sound at you, while showing you my long, sharp teeth. If you still don't back away, I may take a swing at you with my front paws. I hope this doesn't happen often.

If two tom cats are fighting, they can hurt each other. They will scratch and bite, while making deep throaty, growling sounds. Don't try to break them up as you could get hurt in the process. You can throw a little water over them, which usually surprises them and they both run away.

Fighting cats will tear clumps of fur out of each other. In really nasty fights, they can **bite** each other's ears and **scratch** their faces and eyes. Gordon thinks he looks very fierce!

When something frightens me, I try to make myself look as big as possible. I **puff up my fur** and **arch my back**. Even my tail looks bigger and scarier than it usually does. My pupils in my eyes also widen, so that I can see better.

If another cat is attacking me, I'll roll on my back. This protects the back of my neck from its **sharp teeth** and lets me get some good **kicks** in with my back legs.

I let another cat know that I don't want to fight by crouching down to make myself look smaller. I'll pull my head back and **flatten my ears** to show that I'm not looking for trouble.

If I am getting **annoyed**, I usually let you know by wagging my tail from side to side. I do this sometimes if someone creeps up behind me. It helps me work out who is there.

If I'm **cornered** with no chance of escape, I will **attack fiercely**. Dogs that chase me often get a faceful of sharp claws to let them know I've had enough.

If I can **climb** to get away from whatever's frightening me, I will. If you're the tallest thing there, I'll even try to climb up you. But be warned, I'll have my claws out because I'm very scared.

When I'm tired

We cats do like our sleep. We need it to recharge our batteries and relax. I can easily curl up and doze for 18 hours a day, and still need a yawn when I wake up!

When I was a wild animal, I needed to sleep to save energy so that I was always ready to hunt my food. As a pet, I don't need to hunt, but I still like to snooze! Sometimes I doze with my eyes half open. Other times I close them completely but am not sleeping deeply, so can wake if something startles me.

When I was a **very small kitten**, I slept nearly all day and all night. This meant that when mum went off for food, I stayed **safely in the nest** until she came back.

I look for many cosy places around the house to sleep in. I love **warm, dark** spots like airing cupboards. I will crawl into a warm tumble dryer or washing machine. Make sure you check that I'm not inside before you switch it on. I'll often jump on to the spot that you've been sitting on and try to **snooze** there if it's warm. Watch out for me before you sit down, or I might get squashed.

I love to climb and crawl inside things. A sleep hammock is perfect for this. In the winter it can be kept over a radiator. That way I'm toasty warm and comfy all day long.

I'll snooze in **warm, sunny** spots in the garden. **Ledges** are great so that I can look down on what's happening.

If I get too hot, I'll find a cooler spot to snooze in. I'll have favourite places and you'll get used to seeing me there.

My cousins Cecil, Sidney, Philippa and Gemma love to share any bed together.

You can buy me comfy, warm beds from **pet shops**, but I really like to sleep with you in your **bed**. If you want me to have my own bed, you can make one out of a **cardboard box**. Cut a hole in one side so that I can crawl in and make sure it's got plenty of **soft bedding**.

Washing and grooming

When I was a very small kitten, my mum licked me to keep me clean. Her rough tongue raked through my fur and tickled my skin. She made sure I was clean and tidy, so that my fur would keep me warm. By washing me, Mummy spread my scent all along my body. This helped her recognise me as one of her own.

Keeping clean is very important as I pick up unwelcome visitors, like fleas, when I'm out and about. Mummy gets them too. By keeping as clean as possible we can keep down the number of fleas and ticks on our bodies.

You can help too. Wash my bedding from time to time and clean my fur off the places I sleep. This gets rid of any eggs the fleas might have laid.

Grooming helps get rid of loose hair. If I swallow too much hair, it can make a ball in my tummy. I'm often sick to get rid of that!

I've got fairly long hair so it helps me out if you **brush** me every few days. Use a fine-toothed comb or a small, soft brush. You can check that I haven't got fleas at the same time.

Long-haired cats like Persians have fine hair. They need brushing **every day** to stop their hair getting **tangled** and **matted**.

If you find big clumps of matted hair in any cat's fur, ask an adult to cut it out with some round-ended scissors.

I love being groomed and will wriggle around so that the brush can tickle me. Be careful not to whack me in the face if I'm moving around!

Now I'm learning to **wash myself**. I keep my face clean by **licking** the inside edge of my **paw** and rubbing it with that.

Keeping healthy

I'm usually very healthy, but sometimes I get ill. If I go outside a lot, I'll probably meet other cats so it's a good idea to get me vaccinated against certain illnesses that could kill me. The vet will usually do this when I'm a kitten, but some injections are needed every year.

If I go off my food, or seem very limp and sleepy, please take me to the vet.

Usually when I'm sick, it's because I'm trying to get rid of a furball. I eat some grass first and that makes me sick. The fur can get stuck in my tummy and make me constipated. I may need to go to the vet.

If I go outside and hunt, I may swallow tiny worms that can live inside me. These can give me **diarrhoea** and make me **vomit**. My tummy will also look **pot-bellied**. I need tablets to help me get rid of the **worms**.

If I've been fighting, I may have been bitten, especially around my neck or the base of my tail. Bites can get **infected** and become abscesses. You can bathe them in hand-hot, lightly salted water. If the abscess doesn't burst within about 24 hours, take me to the **vet** for a course of **antibiotics**.

If I'm having trouble breathing, sneezing a lot and have a very runny nose, I might have cat flu. This can be very serious, so take me to the vet immediately.

You'll know when my **teeth** need cleaning because my breath will smell really bad! I'll have to go to the vet to have my teeth **cleaned**. He has to make me go to sleep so that he can clean my mouth.

You can buy flea collars and special powders to help get rid of fleas and ticks.

Pleased to meet you!

I like having other animals to play with when you're not around. I can live happily with other cats, especially if I've grown up with them. It's usually best to introduce me to other animals when we are all very young. That way we can all get to know each other, and any squabbles we have will be over before we're grown up. Julia, Ivan, Norman, Frank and Rosie are my best friends.

Don't forget though, that I'm a hunter and may take a swipe at my friends in a moment of madness. Don't leave us alone together for too long.

I can make **friends** with **guinea pigs** and **rabbits** if we meet when we are all babies.

I love having a **dog** to boss around. I can swipe at his legs when he walks past me. Big dogs can be a bit scary, so again, it's best if we all meet up when we're young.

I may not like all of **your friends**, especially if they are very noisy or want to play with me when I'm sleeping. I'll let you know when it's a good time to say hello. If I hiss at you, it means go away.

I get on well with my brothers and sisters, particularly if all us toms are **neutered**. We tend to get **rough** and **fight** if we aren't neutered.

Goodbye!

I've loved writing this book;
I hope it's helped you understand
what makes me happy!

Luca

FIND OUT MORE

Some useful websites:

www.pdsa.org.uk

www.bbc.co.uk/cbbc/wild/pets

www.cats.org.uk

All images © DK except the following:
© Classet: 3, 5bl, 6 main, 7br, 8t, 9tl, 10 main, 11br, 12 main, 15cr,
16 main, 17tl, 18 main, 28 main.
© Corel: 6br, 15tl.
© FPLA: 13tr+cl, 20main, 21cr.
© Getty images: 24 main.